This book belongs to:

A catalogue record for this book is available from the British Library

Published by Ladybird Books Ltd
80 Strand London WC2R 0RL
A Penguin Company

2 4 6 8 10 9 7 5 3 1
© LADYBIRD BOOKS LTD MMVIII
LADYBIRD and the device of a Ladybird are trademarks of Ladybird Books Ltd

ISBN: 978-1-84646-819-3

Printed in China

My best book about... Cars

Written by Stella Maidment
Illustrated by Katie Saunders

Look at all the cars in this busy town!
How many can you count?

Cool Kids

SALE

OPEN

Purrfect Pets

Cars are made in factories –
by people and by robots.
What is happening in this factory?

The brand new cars are loaded on to a transporter. Only two cars are the same. Which two?

The cars go to a showroom to be sold. This man doesn't like blue cars or red cars. Which one should he buy?

Soon all the cars have new owners.
Can you help this car find its home?

People want cars the right size for their families. Can you match these people to their cars?

Racing drivers want cars that can go very fast.

Can you find five differences
between these two pictures?

Sometimes people just want cars that look good!

Where are these cars going?

All cars need to be looked after. What is happening at this busy petrol station?

Cars come in many shapes and sizes.
Can you match each car to its shadow?

Cars have changed a lot over the years. One of these cars is a hundred years old! Which one do you think it is?

In the future cars will probably change again! What do you think they will be like when you're grown up?